REINCAI

Exceptional Cases
Of
Past Life Memories

By <u>Eirik Leivsson</u>

Table of Contents

Legal Notice

The trademarks that are used in this work are without any consent, and the publication of the trademark is without permission or backing by the trademark owner. All trademarks and brands within this book are for clarifying purposes only and are fully owned by the owners themselves, not affiliated with this document.

Respective authors own all copyrights not held by the publisher.

The information herein is offered for informational purposes solely, and is universal as so. The presentation of the information is without contract or any type of guarantee assurance.

In no way is it legal to reproduce, duplicate, or transmit any part of this document in either electronic means or in printed format. Recording of this publication is strictly prohibited and any storage of this document is not allowed unless with written permission from the publisher.

<u>Introduction</u>

*"As a man casting off worn out
garments taketh new ones,
so the dweller in the body entereth
into ones that are new."*

— Epictetus

A four-year-old boy tugs at his mother's dress. "Look Mom! A blue car, just like I used to drive." He points at a Volkswagen Beetle across the road.

"Oh, sweetie. You just had a dream, that's all." She responds, smiling at him.

"No, I did have a car like that! I did. When I was big..."

Such remarks have been made by very young children from all over the world. Of course, such statements may easily be attributed to a child's colorful imagination, or the inability to properly separate dreams from consensus reality. However, while most people would probably dismiss such claims on the spot, what if one actually followed up on what the child was saying? Could it be that a portion of these children actually *are* remembering moments from a different life?

During the course of this book we will explore numerous cases where such claims were indeed investigated, often by serious-minded researchers. And — as you will see — there is evidently more to some of these stories than the mere conjurations of a child's imaginative mind. In fact — as mind blowing as it may be to some — these accounts seem to provide evidence for reincarnation as an actual, real phenomenon.

Is the reductionist materialist model of our reality inaccurate? Are we actually spiritual beings with great potential for evolution, refining our being over countless lifetimes?

Whatever your opinion of these ideas, this book may cause you to think twice about the fascinating concept of reincarnation.

Chapter 1:

<u>A Brief History of Reincarnation</u>

A Quick Overview

Before we delve into specific cases of past life memories, I'd like to first take you on a brief foray into the history and culture of the idea of multiple lives. The concept of reincarnation is one with a rich and deep history, spanning across a number of different cultures and belief structures around the world.

Crude understandings of the phenomenon appeared as early as the ancient pagan faiths, as well as in classical Greek *Presocratic* culture. The mysterious Celtic druids were also believed to have included some form of reincarnation in their view of existence. However, as their traditions are mostly shrouded in mystery, there is some contention as to whether or not this was actually the case.

While the origins of the belief are somewhat obscure, reincarnation as we now have come to recognize it seems to have originated in the cultures of the far east. The earliest commonly accepted instances of this concept being taught comes from the Puranic age with the *Purans* of India. In the Indo-Aryan texts are where we see the concept of reincarnation gain real, significant popularity. This Hindu text

3

spoke of *Punarjunma* — which translates loosely to rebirth — and of *Punarmrytu,* which essentially means re-death. It's with texts such as these that we see a real blossoming of the concept throughout earlier Eastern cultures.

There were many societies that followed this initial transition into what we now recognize as soul transmigration, including Buddhism and Judaism with the Zohar in the 13th century, which covered the concept at length. The Taoist during the Han Dynasty also mentioned many lives in their teachings. Norse mythology is also worth mentioning, as the deities had something that we would recognize as reincarnation. And finally, into the 19th century we see philosophers such as Schopenhauer and Nietzche, who took a more secular approach to the concept.

While the belief has endured into the modern age in popular faiths such as Hinduism, Buddhism, Taoism and several New-Age groups, there has also been a more scientific approach to dealing with the question as to whether or not such a thing as reincarnation can actually be verified. The first in the 20th century to take this route was one William James — who was an American philosopher, physician and psychologist.

More recently, in the past 40 years or so, there have been a number of experiments and research initiatives taking place in the Western world regarding the phenomenon. To understand this modern inquiry into reincarnation, there is one person in particular who we need to be aware of. A person who — when it comes to past life memories — has had an invaluable role in shaping the landscape of knowledge as it stands today.

A Pioneer of Past Life Research:

The work of Dr. Ian Stevenson

As of today, most fields of study that are considered "supernatural" are rarely granted any notable funding for extensive research, and reincarnation tends to be put in that category. Still, there have been a few prominent figures who tried to uncover some of the mystery behind this phenomenon using carefully devised research methods. The most notable among them was Dr. Ian Stevenson.

An ambitious psychiatrist

Ian Stevenson was born on October 31, 1918 in Montreal, Canada. He studied medicine at the St. Andrews University from 1937 to 1939, but had to complete his studies in Canada because of the Second World War. During his career as a physician, he took a special interest in psychosomatic disorders (diseases involving both mind and body). He began thinking outside — what he considered to be — the reductionist boundaries of practiced biochemistry, and eventually he switched disciplines to psychiatry.

During the early 1950s, he met the famed writer and philosopher, Aldous Huxley. Stevenson, fascinated by the meeting, became encouraged to further delve into the uncharted areas of the human mind. He began exploring the true origins of individuals' characteristics and the development of personality. The popular view at the time was that personality became fixed in early childhood, but he felt this was — at best — an incomplete theory. Eventually, he took notice of various accounts of young children who claimed to have memories from previous lives.

In 1960, he published a paper titled *The Evidence for Survival from Claimed Memories of Former Incarnations*. This caught the attention of Chester Carlson, the inventor of the photocopier (Xerox), and his spiritually inclined wife. Carlson funded Stevenson's first field trips to India and Sri Lanka in 1961, where he studied 25 possible reincarnation cases.

Eventually, Stevenson was appointed chairman of the department of psychiatry at the University of Virginia. He started doing more mainstream work and put his unorthodox research on the sideline. In 1968, Chester Carlson died of a sudden heart attack. In his will he had left 1 million dollars to the University of Virginia, under the instructions that the money was to be used to fund parapsychology research. Carlson's posthumous donation enabled Stevenson to continue his research into reincarnation. He established the *Division of Personality Studies*, a department dedicated to the study of previous lives, near-death experiences and other paranormal phenomena.

The journey continues

With the monetary backing secured, Stevenson was reinvigorated, and was now eager to continue his investigation. In the years that followed, he spent enormous amounts of time travelling in South America, Lebanon, West Africa and South-East Asia. In his earlier days of conducting field research, most of his cases were found in countries where there existed some form of belief system which included reincarnation. Early on, this fact was frequently used by skeptics to try to discredit his work. Stevenson was of the opinion that doing research in these areas were more fruitful because the children's stories were taken more seriously, and therefore investigated more frequently by the parents.

In most Western cultures at the time, both the Christian and the materialist/reductionist mindset were mostly inhospitable environments for past life recollection in children, as such claims were more likely to be dismissed immediately as vivid fantasy. Still, Stevenson did conduct research in the West towards the end of his career, coinciding with the rising acceptance of the concept in this part of the world.

Common features

Most of the cases Ian Stevenson studied had several features in common, which he learned to look for:

1. <u>In about 50 % of the studied cases, a violent, tragic or premature death occurred in the alleged previous incarnation.</u>

 For some reason, children who ended their previous life in a dramatic fashion seem to remember much more details, as well as spending less time in the state between incarnations. Furthermore, Dr. Stevenson noted that people who reportedly died from traumatic wounds — more often than not — had corresponding birthmarks where the wounds were made on the body. For example, one man who killed himself with a gunshot to the head, had reincarnated as a boy with birthmarks under his chin and on the top of his head — lining up perfectly with the trajectory of the bullet.

Another man — who said he was killed by an assailant with a shotgun — had a large, unusual birthmark in the middle of his chest which looked like — and matched the placement of — the deadly wound on the deceased person's body.

2. <u>As soon as the child can communicate, it starts to relay information about the previous life.</u>

At a very young age, the child may speak of his "other" or "real" parents, call itself by another name and/or mention several past family members, close friends and specific geographic locations by name.

3. <u>Based on information given by the child, the former family from the previous incarnation is identified.</u>

When the child is reunited with the former family in the current life, the child can identify them either by name or by relationship. In many cases, the child will form a long-term relationship with the former family while primarily staying with the new one.

4. <u>Physical appearance is similar between incarnations.</u>

Several cases clearly demonstrated how the facial structure can remain quite consistent from one life to another. It is uncertain if this is the case for everyone, or if this is another phenomenon related to an intense death experience (like the birth marks and birth defects). In some instances, photographs were even available for side by side comparison, and obvious likeness could be clearly seen.

5. Personality traits and habits may continue.

For example, a notable affinity for certain foods or beverages may persist between incarnations. The child may also show interest and great skill in dealing with objects or activities which were a major part of its previous life experience. This may be one explanation of so-called child prodigies.

6. Former relationships are continued through reincarnation.

Dr. Stevenson did a large study on 31 sets of twins, whose past lives had been sufficiently validated. In all of these cases, the twins had significant relationships in their previous incarnations.

The end (?)

Dr. Ian Stevenson died of pneumonia in February, 2007, at his retirement home in Charlottesville, Virginia. During his career, he investigated around 2500 reports of children who told of memories from a past life. In approximately 1200 of these cases, Stevenson was able to collect sufficient data to validate the child's claims. Stevenson has — without a doubt — been one of the most influential in the field of parapsychology, and has played a very important role in paving the way for future researchers of reincarnation and past life memories in children.

Chapter 2:

Stories from the West

"A little while,
a moment of rest upon the wind,
and another woman shall bear me."

— Kahlil Gibran, "The Prophet"

The belief in reincarnation is mainly found in countries of the far east. These are places where children's past life memories are more often accepted and even encouraged, thus we are more likely to find such stories from these areas. This is the main reason why most of the cases of past life memory — up to very recently — have been investigated there.

As mentioned, this fact was often used by skeptics to criticize the work of Dr. Ian Stevenson and his colleagues. Nevertheless — as Stevenson quickly discovered — there are children from all over the world who are reporting memories of past lives. This also includes the mostly Christian or secular countries of the Western world.

Case 1: The Boy Who Flew

Carl Edon was born in Middlesbrough, England, on December 29, 1972. His parents were Valerie and James Edon. Carl had a brother, eleven years older than him, and a sister who was five years older. As opposed to the rest of his family — who all had dark brown hair — Carl was extremely blond and had clear blue eyes. As soon as he was able to speak somewhat coherently at two years of age, he began talking about crashing a plane. Eventually, he added more details to the story; that he was on a bombing mission over England and that he lost his right leg in the crash. Coincidentally, he had a large birthmark at the area where he claimed his leg was torn off in the collision.

After learning to use a pencil, he immediately began creating sketches of swastikas and eagles of a particular, consistent style. Carl was very talented at drawing intricate pictures, even as a child. At the age of six he drew the whole panel of an airplane's cockpit, and proceeded to describe the functions of the gauges to his parents. Carl would also spontaneously perform movements such as the characteristic Nazi salute and the infamous goose-step march.

When standing up he was always erect, and mostly kept his hands at his sides. When the family were watching films which included German soldiers, Carl would make passing comments about the vehicles which were used, or how the German uniforms were wrongly portrayed. Furthermore, he frequently expressed a strong wish to travel to Germany and live there.

Dr. Ian Stevenson was informed of the case after one of his

English colleagues had discovered Carl's story through some associates. He personally travelled to England, where he carefully observed Carl, and conducted interviews with both him and his parents. While investigating the case, Stevenson explored several possible leads in order to find a match for Carl's recollections, but came up short. A wreckage containing three Nazi pilots had indeed been recovered near Middlesbrough, around where Carl said he went down. However, neither the crash site nor any of the three bodies matched the description of his story.

Stevenson stated that he reached the case a bit late for his liking, noting that the strongest cases were when he contacted the family when the child's memories were still fresh, and therefore, more lucid. Additionally, Carl's parents — who were both Christian — had not kept notes about the details of his earliest memories. They were initially very skeptical and uncomfortable regarding Carl's incredible statements, but eventually came to accept his experiences as real.

After his case was published in the local newspaper, Carl's schoolmates started teasing him and calling him a Nazi. This treatment went on for some time, and at around ten or eleven years of age, Carl stopped speaking about his past life memories. When Stevenson revisited Carl Edon in 1993, Carl (now 21 years old) seemed to have forgotten most of his memories from the previous incarnation.

While Ian Stevenson never succeeded in verifying Carl's story of the plane crash, the case was later picked up by a local historian, who uncovered some startling information. A plane wreckage was unearthed near Middlesbrough in 1997, and the body of a Nazi pilot — whose leg was severed (just as in Carl's recollection) — was recovered. The name of the man was Heinrich Richter, who in 1942 was on a mission in a German

Dornier bomber plane with three crew members, before being shot down by British anti-aircraft guns. The bodies of the other three pilots were recovered after the crash, but the wreckage containing Richter was in a separate location, which resulted in his remains not being discovered until much later.

Unfortunately, Carl never got to witness the discovery of his potentially former incarnation. In 1995, just 2 years before the discovery of Richter's body, a rather eerie twist of fate took place. While working at a train depot in Skinningrove, east of his hometown, he was suddenly attacked by his colleague, Gary Vinter. Vinter had a long history of violence and would later end up killing his own wife. He violently stabbed Carl 37 times, which resulted in all of his vital organs being punctured, and finally, his death.

Thus, Carl Edon's life ended in the village of Skinningrove. Coincidentally, this turned out to be the very same village which Heinrich Richter had bombed over 40 years earlier, right before heading towards Carl's birthplace of Middlesbrough, where he was shot down.

Case 2: Traces of the Tribe

A healthy and seemingly normal boy was born in Budapest, Hungary, on March 7, 1921. His parents — Elisabeth Haich and her husband, Subo — named him Gedeon. Their marriage would not last long, as they divorced when Gedeon was around three years old. He lived with his mother for the next four years before his father obtained formal custody of him when he was seven. Gedeon spent the remainder of his childhood with him, but frequently visited his mother throughout the year in addition to spending his summers with her.

Unlike most children who recall previous lives, Gedeon did not spontaneously begin speaking about his memories as soon as he learned to talk. At around four years of age, however, his mother noticed something odd one day while Gedeon and his female cousin were drawing pictures together. For some inexplicable reason, when they were drawing human figures, Gedeon would color all of his characters dark brown. Quite an unusual thing to do for a young Hungarian boy of the 1920s, to say the least. Some of his drawings included exotic landscapes and animals as well. Later, he drew a picture of — what he claimed to be — himself using a bow and arrow to hunt some type of bird that was sitting in a palm tree. He drew himself with dark skin as well.

One day — when Gedeon was around six years old — he asked his mother directly whether he might have lived somewhere else, before he became her son. Being quite surprised by his unusual question, his mother asked him what made him think of such an idea. He replied that he remembered being in a different country with different people, where he had a wife and children. He added that when he was waking up in his bed in the morning, with his eyes still closed, he sometimes thought that he was still a grown man in a tropical environment. When he opened his eyes and looked around, however, he remembered that he was now a small boy — Elisabeth's son.

When Elisabeth further questioned him about his family, he said:

"My wife and children and the other people there are not like people here; they are all black and almost naked."

His mother then asked Gedeon where he lived. He quickly grabbed a pencil and some paper, and drew a picture of a hut with a cone shaped roof, with a small vent in the top. In front of the hut he drew a naked, dark skinned woman with long breasts, and next to the hut he made a wide river covered with waves. Gedeon explained that the woman in his drawing was his "dear wife". When Elisabeth asked why he drew his wife with such long, hanging, ugly breasts, Gedeon became noticeably offended. He told his mother that his wife's breasts were not ugly at all — and that his wife was indeed very beautiful.

As if his memories had been spurred, he went on to tell his mother a story which made her a bit startled. He explained that he had been out in the wilderness hunting one day, and threw his spear at what looked like a tiger — wounding it — but failing to kill it. The last memory he had was a moment of intense fear, and the furious animal pouncing on him with all of its weight.

In addition to these extraordinary remarks, Gedeon also showed great talent in several activities which could be connected to a tribal lifestyle. The first time he was in a boat with his family, he could row it as if he had been doing it for years, and could easily steer it between other boats. "With my tree boat — where I lived — I could do everything", he said.

He also added that a kind of monster roamed the water where he previously lived, and that it could easily bite people's legs off. A year or so prior to the spurring of Gedeon's recollections, there had been an incident during an outing at their family's summer home — which was located near a lake. When Gedeon was invited to join the family members who were swimming in the lake, he refused to even get near the water. Thinking he was just being silly, Elisabeth grabbed him and tried to carry him with her. Gedeon let out a fearful scream and struggled desperately to get loose, apparently terrified of the water. Nobody could understand Gedeon's fear of the lake. She stated, however, that Gedeon did not have the same reaction when entering man-made swimming pools. Stevenson speculated that Gedeon's strong fear of outdoor waters may have been caused by him being attacked by a crocodile in his previous life.

As Gedeon got older, other strange traits were spontaneously discovered. The boy loved — and was extremely efficient at— climbing all sorts of trees. At the age of 13, he scaled an 82 ft. high poplar tree, much to the dismay of his mother. When he was 15, his mother purchased a large jazz drum, which he had wanted for a long time. On the very day he received it, he demonstrated excellent skill in playing highly complicated rhythms on the drum. After playing a rather unusual rhythm, he said:

"Do you see, Mama? This is the way we could send signals and messages to each other over great distances."

As noted by Dr. Ian Stevenson, because Gedeon's alleged past incarnation as a tribal man could not be specifically identified in any conceivable way, his story could not be historically validated. However, all of the details Gedeon provided strongly implied a connection to some sort of African tribal community. Dark skinned people wearing little clothing, large drums, crocodiles in the water, palm trees, spears and bows, dugout boats and round huts with conical roofs. The only detail which seems to be unfitting is the story of the animal he threw the spear at. At a young age, Gedeon saw a tiger in a zoo and pointed it out as the animal that jumped on him, yet tigers are native to Asia and are not found in Africa. It may very well be that he was actually talking about a lion or — more likely — a leopard. Additionally, before and after the visit to the zoo, he referred to it only as "the beast" and not tiger specifically.

Although the memories of his past life got blurrier as he grew older, and eventually faded, Gedeon kept his strong affinity to Africa throughout his life.

Case 3: Tomboy

Taru Järvi was born in Helsinki, Finland, on May 27, 1976. Her parents were Heikki Järvi and his wife, Iris. Taru began speaking of a past life very early, at around one and a half years of age. She initially rejected the name Taru and told her mother her actual name was Jaska. This just so happened to be the nickname of Iris' Järvi's ex-husband, Jaako Vuorenlehto, who had been run over and killed by a bus three years earlier.

When questioned, Taru did indeed mention being hit by a vehicle. When asked about the size of this vehicle, Taru said: "It was big. First died the stomach, then the head." She also added: "I was taken to the hospital, but I was already dead by that time." Stevenson's research later showed this to be an accurate description of Jaako's death. As a child, Taru had a notable fear of buses and other large vehicles. So much so that she would ask her mother to pick her up whenever a bus came their way.

Since birth, Taru had showed clear aversion towards her father, Heikki. She once told her father:

"We do not need you here, you should go away."

On another occasion she remarked:

"You shouldn't live here with us. You are only a visitor."

Taru was Heikki's only child, and this dismissive attitude hurt him deeply. Taru's continued rejection of her father led to a partial separation between Iris and Heikki. They lived in separate houses during fall and winter, but during the summer they would live together in a cottage at the countryside.

Like other girls, Taru would play with dolls. However, she was more interested in toy soldiers, guns and cars. When playing together with other children, she would reject the girl's part if they were doing role-plays, insisting that she was a boy. On several occasions, Taru would claim that she "used to be a big man." She also had a strong preference for boy's clothes and accessories. Growing up, she never wore any makeup, and was always dressed in pants. Jaako's mother (Taru's grandmother) and Iris both noticed a close similarity in facial features between Taru and Jaako. Additionally — as Taru grew older — she became very tall and quite clumsy in her movements, just as Jaako had been. Taru actually grew to be taller than her father.

According to her mother, Taru was "still masculine" at the age of 23. She worked as a taxi driver and managed a stable for boarding horses. Despite her rather manly behavior throughout her life, she married a man in 1998 and even wore a skirt for her wedding. As Taru matured — and got increasingly comfortable with her new identity — she became more and more accepting of her father, Heikki. As he became older and frailer, Taru helped take care of him, and — before he passed on — she finally gave him the affection he had longed for since she was a child.

From the data he compiled over his career, Dr. Ian Stevenson noted that in most cases of reincarnation, individuals seem to be born the same gender as their previous persona. Examples such as this one, where gender is changed at birth, usually involve a person of above-average intelligence. This may suggest that the ability to effortlessly switch between genders is a trait of more highly evolved "souls".

Furthermore, as Stevenson has pointed out — and we have observed in the cases we have looked at so far — a sudden, traumatic or highly emotional ending to a life is usually the precursor to experiencing past life memories during the next incarnation, as well as having varying degrees of behavioral carryover. This would explain Taru's unmistakably masculine features. As Jaako Vuorenlehto was abruptly killed by the bus, some of his memories and traits could have carried over into the next incarnation, where these then manifested as different manly features in the new female form.

Could this be an explanation for why some people are born with varying degrees of gender dysphoria?

Case 4: Return

Eeva-Maija Kaartinen was born on August 17, 1923 in Oulu, a city in the northern part of Finland. She lived together with her two parents and three brothers. Already from a very young age, Eeva seemed to differentiate herself from the rest of her family. While her parents and siblings preferred to drink sour milk and eat meat, Eeva would refuse to consume these items. Instead, Eeva liked to drink fresh milk and eat fish. Mostly, however, she was unenthusiastic about eating in general. She would take ages to finish her dinner, being the last one to leave the dinner table, and would even try to hide some of the food so that she wouldn't have to eat it. Her mother usually had to feed her, and would coach Eeva by repeating the words, "Eat, bite, swallow."

Eeva was quite physical when expressing herself, and loved to dance. Even before she could walk properly, she would swing her body to the rhythm of any music that was playing. When she was around four and a half years of age, she learned to do "The Charleston", a dance which was very prominent in the 1920's.

Soon after reaching five years of age, Eeva-Maija began showing signs of ill health. She spent a lot of time bedridden, with a high fever, stuffy nose and a horrible cough. The doctors advised Eeva's parents that she had come down with a serious case of influenza. Her mother — devastated by her daughter's vulnerable state — promised Eeva that she would buy her a toy baby carriage that she could play with when she got well again.

Unfortunately, the influenza proved to be too much to handle for Eeva's five-year-old body. She passed away in her sleep on November 24, 1928. Salli, Eeva's mother, was three months pregnant at the time of her death. Six months later, on May 22 of 1929, she gave birth to another girl. The child was named Marja-Liisa. According to Salli, Marja-Liisa and Eeva-Majia looked almost exactly the same, noting that the only difference was that Eeva had been blonde while Marja was a brunette.

It didn't take long before this newly arrived girl started to behave in anomalous ways. As early as the age of two — when she first started speaking — she would insist on being called Eeva. When she discovered photographs of Eeva-Maija, she would show the photos to people and tell them, "These are of me".

Like Eeva, Marja refused to consume the sour milk and the meat that her family preferred. She favored the fish and fresh milk instead. And, just like Eeva, Marja was acting very averse towards eating her food in general. One day, she told her mother, "Mom, why don't you say to me what you told Eeva, eat, bite, swallow?" Salli was stunned by Marja's remark. When interview by Dr. Ian Stevenson, she mentioned that all members of the Kaartinen family had agreed to not talk about Eeva-Maija after her untimely death, in an attempt to ease her deep sorrow for her lost child. Thus, Marja's question was perceived as eerie and mysterious to the family.

Marja showed a great deal of attachment to Eeva's belongings. For example, she would rather wear the clothes of (technically) her deceased sister, than wear the new items which were bought for her. She behaved exactly the same way with her toys. When Marja-Liisa reached the age of three, the Kaartinen family travelled to their summer cabin in Sotkomo – a small municipality in the center part of Finland. Upon arriving, Marja asked her parents, "Where is Helim?". Helim was a man who previously worked as the family's servant. He had left the Kaartinens' employment a year prior to Marja's birth. According to Salli, no one had mentioned Helim to Marja.

At the back of the family's summer cabin, there was a container which stored various toys. As soon as Marja arrived at the cabin, she went straight towards the container and then picked out all of Eeva-Maija's toys, while leaving the ones which belonged to the other children of the family. Among these were one of four different balls and one of two different dolls.

Marja also showed a great love for music, and — just like Eeva — began dancing before she could even walk properly. Most intriguing was the fact that — when her mother played the piano one day — Marja spontaneously began to dance "The Charleston". Marja had never learned this dance. Eeva, on the other hand, had practiced the routine extensively when she was alive. This took place when she was still under the age of four. As with many other cases of past life memory, such a specific, unexplained talent in a young child seems to be connected with a skill that was practiced in a previous lifetime.

At the age of four, Marja asked her mother, "Where were we...when Peter Pan flew?". It turned out that she was speaking about the 1924 silent adventure film "Peter Pan", by Paramount Pictures, which Salli had watched together with

Eeva when she was alive. Marja, however, had never seen the movie.

Around the age of five, a highly emotional moment occurred when — out of nowhere — Marja asked her mother about the baby carriage that she promised to buy for her. This promise, as you may remember, was not made to Marja, but rather to the dying Eeva-Maija.

Suffice it to say, the family was convinced that Marja was the reincarnation of their deceased daughter, Eeva. Although not directly mentioned in Stevenson's research, one may assume that the members of the Kaartinen family — especially the mother, Salli — found great peace in this realization.

Case 5: Fragments of the Past

As opposed to the other cases we have looked at so far, the following story does not include a young child's recollection of past life memories. Instead, Peter Avery — the subject of this story — had memories vividly reignited when he was exposed to an environment from a supposed previous incarnation.

You may have had moments in your own life where a sensation — most often a smell — brought back a clear memory from your past. This was also the case with Peter Avery. However, instead of reliving a moment from his childhood or teenage years, he was brought back to a completely forgotten time. A different life. A different *him*.

Peter Avery was born in Derby, England, on May 15, 1923. He had a relatively normal childhood, with no clear signs (at least none that were acknowledged by his parents) of past life memory recollection. It was not until he reached 21 years of age, in 1944, that anomalies would start to emerge. When the Second World War was raging, Avery was stationed with the Royal Indian Navy. One day, an Indian officer invited him to meet his family in Lahore, which today is considered as the cultural heart of Pakistan. The officer had been informed of Peter's marked interest in Islamic culture and literature, and wanted him to meet his father — who was a respected scholar of Islamic history. Peter — thrilled by the opportunity — agreed to go with him.

When they reached Lahore, they met with the officer's father, Bahadur Muhammad Shafi, who took them on a tour to the *Shalimar Bagh,* a garden compound that was constructed during the reign of the Mughal empire (a Muslim Persianate dynasty of Turco-Mongol origin that stretched over large parts of India and Afghanistan). There, he guided them around every part of the building, explaining the history as they walked along. Avery and Bahadur entered the complex through a special opening in an encircling wall. Somehow, Peter perceived that this was not the initial entryway of the Shalimar Bagh, and told Bahadur that the original entrance was on the opposite side of the courtyard. Bahadur told him that his statement was correct. This intuitive knowledge baffled Avery himself, who had not previously visited the Shalimar Bagh, He had not even seen any pictures or read about the structure.

Later in the day, Peter remarked that a small building in the middle of the garden was not part of the original layout of the complex. Bahadur once again confirmed Peter's assertion, adding that the building was initially part of an emperor's gravesite, but was relocated to the garden by a Sikh lord who governed Lahore in the period of 1799-1839.

After a pleasant and informative stay in Lahore, Peter bid farewell to Bahadur and returned to his military station together with his colleague. He pondered on the eerie nature of his sudden, intuitive recognition about the Shalimar Bagh. Could he have overheard something, or read about it in a textbook somewhere, but misplaced the information in his head? It was quite unlike his academic mind to be so disorganized, especially regarding a subject he was so passionate about.

When the war finally ended, Peter went to study at the University of London, where he graduated in 1949 with a degree in Persian and Arabic languages. With his new skills, he was accepted to work for the Anglo-Iranian Oil Company (AIOC), where he acted as Training Manager for Persian and Arabic languages. He was sent to the city of Abadan, located in the southwestern region of Iran. He was restricted to Abadan and its enclosing oil fields for the first six months of his new job.

In 1950, John Evans — a manager from AIOC's London office, was set to tour various facilities in Iran, and needed a skilled interpreter to escort him. Peter Avery was appointed to accompany Mr. Evans on a trip to Isfahan, located in the central part of Iran. Avery — growing weary of his restricted work space — was thrilled by the assignment, as he would like to see other areas of the country.

Once in Isfahan, Peter got another spontaneous, intuitive moment. While they were planning out the trip for the day, he described in detail the route that they would be taking from their hotel to the city's marketplace and onwards to *Maidan-I Shah*, which was a town square that was part of a palace-complex built between 1590-1595. Mr. Evans was impressed by Peter's comprehensive knowledge of the streets of Isfahan. Peter himself, however, could not explain why he knew what he did about the area. He was certain that he had never read any relevant guidebooks or even looked at a map of the region. When they actually walked through the city, Peter's prepared route proved to be completely accurate.

At the end of their tour that day, Peter escorted Mr. Evans to the *Madrasa Mader-e Shah,* a religious complex built in 1706. In the garden of the compound there is a mosque with a blue dome. Immediately upon walking into the courtyard of the Mader-e Shah and seeing this blue-domed mosque, a flood of emotions suddenly came over Peter. He simply couldn't help himself, and burst into tears, under the impression that he had "come home" in a way. Overwhelmed by the sensations, he sat down at the edge of a nearby pool, while Mr. Evans thoughtfully walked away to give him some space.

Avery later noted that — although he himself was greatly embarrassed by the episode — Mr. Evans didn't react in a negative manner. Instead, he acted calm, and seemed to be sympathetic about the situation. Peter was as confused — if not more — than Mr. Evans. Why did he experience such a strong sense of familiarity with a place he never even knew existed?

Moved by the incident, Peter became even more enthralled with Persian culture. He went on to work as a lecturer of Persian studies at Cambridge University in England between 1958 and 1990, before he ended up at the King's College. There, he developed into a well-known and respected scholar of Persian studies, and became recognized for his accurate translations of the Persian poets *Omar Khayyam* and *Hafez.* Furthermore, he wrote thoroughly about Iranian history, from the country's earliest beginnings up until modern times.

When Dr. Ian Stevenson met with Avery in 1992 to discuss his experiences, Avery stated that he had come to perceive his innate knowledge of the foreign land as remnants from a past life. He was, however, open to other explanations, not being fanatical about the idea in any way. An alternate theory he suggested was that of so-called inherited memory. He mentioned that he had an ancestor from the 17th century; a pirate who was known to raid shipping boats in the Indian Ocean. If his plundering forebear ever visited Lahore and Isfahan, though, is unknown. Whatever the case may be, Peter Avery carried these experiences close to his heart until the end of his life. At the age of 85 — after a long period of ill health — he passed away in his home in England, on October 6, 2008. Avery's story is — as mentioned — quite unlike the usual past life memory cases. Although highly intriguing, the nature of his potential recollections were such that no hard evidence could be gathered to validate his perceptions.

To sum up, he had a seemingly innate passion for Islamic and Persian culture, he had an awareness of the earliest design of the Shalimar Burg, he was inexplicably closely familiar with the streets if Isfahan and had an intense emotional reaction inside the Madrasa-e Shah, together with a feeling of having returned home. Though not verified by in-field research — with all things considered — it seems plausible that Peter Avery's strong inclinations towards the foreign cultures, as well as the apparently spontaneous knowledge about various locations and large, intricate structures, stemmed from one or more past lifetimes in Pakistan and Iran.

Chapter 3:

Past Life Regressions

"I look upon death to be as necessary to the constitution as sleep.

We shall rise refreshed in the morning."

- Benjamin Franklin

In this chapter we will take a look at three cases involving past life regressions. Past life regression is a practice which uses hypnosis techniques in order to recover what practitioners perceive are memories from previous incarnations. This is usually thought of as an inferior method when compared to investigating the fragmented memories in-field, and for very good reasons.

As the process of regression is entirely performed with the mind alone, the outcome is completely dependent on the mental skill and focus of both the hypnotist and the hypnotized. It is well known that certain people are more easily able to be effectively hypnotized than others. One person may enter a deep trance in the blink of an eye, while another may only dwell in a shallow hypnotic state where the conscious mind is still present and able to color the experience. Additionally, an unskilled hypnotist could ask suggestive questions which may lead to a distorted reception in the person who is undergoing the regression, or the hypnotist may not even be able to keep a person in a steady trance to begin with.

Thus, there are many variables to consider, which one may argue makes past life regressions unreliable. Nonetheless, there are some cases that stand out as particularly interesting, which are still worth mentioning.

Case 1: The Forgotten Artist

In the case of Robert Snow, we find an individual who had no previous belief in reincarnation or past life memories whatsoever. Snow worked as the head of homicide investigation for the Indianapolis Police Department. He was not a man of faith. In fact, he readily dismissed cases of past life regression and reincarnation as mere hoaxes or wishful thinking. He came to participate in a past life regression initially as an effort to disprove the phenomenon. At work, there was a fellow police officer whom he knew that practiced past life regression hypnosis as a hobby. During a friendly debate, the officer dared Snow to undergo a session himself. On a whim, he agreed, without any real intention of actually participating. As time passed, however, he was goaded into living up to his word.

He entered a session with Dr. Mariellen Griffith with outright skepticism. By his own admission he fought the process of hypnotism for as long as he could, but eventually fell into a hypnotic state where he experienced striking recollections from what looked to be a previous incarnation. Snow found himself speaking unconsciously with the hypnotherapist about a past life. He was generally outside his ability to control the content he was seeing and conveying. He recalled distinct moments of being a struggling painter.

Snow vividly remembered creating his works of art, down to the individual brush strokes. One painting which stood out in particular, was of a hunchbacked woman. He could remember wondering why such a woman would want a portrait to begin with. He also recalled that his wife couldn't have any children due to a medical issue, and that a near and dear relative died of a blood clot. His session finally ended with the memory of his death, in a large city with tall buildings which looked to be from the 1910s.

Though this experience was incredibly vivid and striking, he initially dismissed it as some sort of hypnosis-induced anomaly. However — as time went on — he found that the impressions from the session would not fade. In particular, the potential memories of the paintings he saw became a sort of overwhelming obsession for him, eventually compelling him to investigate it in an effort to disprove this experience. He believed that if he could prove that these paintings didn't exist, then he could dislodge them from his mind and move on. He treated this endeavor like he would any other police investigation, looking into several art sources including a myriad of art books and galleries, but without finding anything. After a while, he laid it to rest, convinced that the paintings in question weren't real.

A year later, however, when he went on a vacation with his wife to New Orleans, he experienced a sudden break in the case. Completely by chance, Snow and his wife wandered into an art gallery in the French Quarter of New Orleans, where he stumbled upon the painting of the hunchbacked woman. The moment was one of complete and utter disbelief, but there it was; right before his eyes, the portrait he had spent so much time and effort searching for. The painting — it turned out — was done by a man named James Carroll Beckwith. With a name to go on, Robert Snow managed to track down a diary and various scrapbooks belonging to Beckwith.

Looking into the life of Carroll Beckwith, Snow found that the memories he had experienced during his regression matched up with facts about Beckwith's life — including the fact that his wife couldn't have kids, having a relative who died of a blood clot as well as several other memories. In total, he had distilled out 28 points from the tape recording of his session with the hypnotist, which could be proven or disproven.

From his investigation of Beckwith's life and personal belongings, Snow was able to provide evidence for 26 of the 28 points. In addition to memories that correspond with Beckwith's actual life, Snow bears a striking physical resemblance to Beckwith; something that is common in past life memory cases that are verified by research. Robert Snow detailed his discoveries regarding his past life memories in his book "Looking for Carroll Beckwith".

Case 2: Sexual Distortion

The next case we are going to look at is the case of Sarah Foster. This case is an example of how past life regression is being practiced as a form of psychological therapy, aimed at helping individuals in areas that traditional medical practices have failed to heal. The concept of past life regression as therapy is a relatively new idea, but has been known to produce beneficial results for some people.

The story of 23- year-old Sarah Foster is a rather unique one. Prior to turning to past life regression therapy, she had tried several different medical and psychological treatments in an effort to sooth the intense anxiety that accompanied her orgasms. Regardless of partners or circumstances, the moment before climax was always met with much pain and distress. As a result, she had developed an intense fear of intimacy that hindered her ability to pursue any sort of romantic or sexual relationship. In addition to her issues with intimacy, she also experienced a strange pain that would frequently spring up when she was sleeping — waking her up around 4 AM several days during the week.

Sarah's past life regression therapy was performed by one Dr. Morris Netherton, an experienced hypnotherapist who had performed hundreds of past life regressions. Sarah was initially skeptical as to whether or not this unorthodox approach would help, but was willing to try anything to achieve some level of relief at this point.

The regression initially sent Sarah to an apparent past life where she was in a remote African village. She was in a cage — confined by someone who she recognized to be her husband — as some form of punishment for infidelity. She had been confined for days in a space so small that she was forced to crouch to sleep, and the pain in her abdomen was excruciating. It was on this day (that she had regressed to) that her husband and another man dragged her out of the cage and out to a remote area in the woods. Once they reached a clearing, she was brutally beaten with a cat-o'-nine-tails whip.

When reliving this traumatic experience, she physically thrashed on the therapy couch, and her therapist reported seeing welts appear on her cheek, shoulders and chin. More physical signs may have been emerging under her clothes as well. Thankfully, these physical manifestations of her mental distress receded as the session progressed. Further along in the session, she found herself once again squatting in her cage, pleading with her husband to be released. She told him she would do anything for him to show mercy. After a time, he finally relented.

She vividly remembered being removed from the small cage and being bathed. She recalled how amazing the warm water felt, feeling as if the nightmare had finally come to an end. She couldn't imagine how wrong she was. After the bath, she remembers being handed a drink which she eagerly chugged down. She overheard her husband and a man — whom appeared to be a doctor of some sort — talking about how the drink was for the pain. "What pain?" she thought, as she was quickly filled by dread, thinking about what horrible fate could be in store for her.

Suddenly, she got drowsy until the point that she could barely walk. She was then lead away to a room and laid down. The next thing she remembers was an extremely sharp pain in her vaginal area which was so intense that she passed out. What she was remembering having experienced was the gruesome practice of female genital mutilation. In this procedure, some or all of the external female genitalia is removed with a blade, which largely stops the female from deriving pleasure from sexual intercourse. This is still carried out in several African countries to this day, where girls as young as ten years old are mangled in this manner.

Sarah Foster's next memory is of her having recovered from the ordeal. Her husband is pleased with himself, feeling he has solved the issue of her infidelity. He uses her for sex frequently, without giving her any degree of love or comfort. This new dynamic has left her with a sense of feeling like less than a human being. She feels helplessly trapped. Her depression grows by the day and she thinks of suicide frequently. Finally, one day, she can take it no longer. She breaks down mentally and grabs a very sharp knife which she drives violently into her abdomen. Sarah remembered an incredible pain unlike anything she'd ever felt before. The world was slowly slipping away as she bled out. In her last moments, she could remember thinking, "All I wanted was to be loved..."

After the hypnosis session ended, Sarah and Dr. Netherton discussed the experience, and drew some parallels between the apparent past incarnation in Africa and her present life's experience with past boyfriends. More often than not, she had been mentally controlled by her partners, and had always wondered why she allowed herself to be abused to such a degree.

After taking some time off — reflecting over the stunning revelations — Sarah and Dr. Netherton agreed to schedule another session. When she entered the trance state this second time, she found herself transitioning into a different life than the last one. In this incarnation, she found herself in early America sometime during the early western expansion. She worked mainly as a bar waitress, but earned some extra cash as a prostitute. She had worked there since she was quite young — perhaps late teens — and was relatively inexperienced.

She felt herself being pulled aside by what was obviously a client, and taken upstairs. This man was more gentle and loving than most, and she felt herself enjoying herself almost as if they were making love. However, before she could reach climax, he was done, and stopped the session without giving her another thought. On top of that, he made an insulting remark about her sexual performance as he put some money on the nightstand before leaving.

She went from euphoria to crying, wondering why no one ever loved her. She left the room in a sort of mental haze. While attempting to descend the stairs, she tripped and fell, tumbling down the entire flight of stairs and bashing her head on the bottom banister. She was helped upstairs and placed into a bed without receiving any kind of medical attention whatsoever, even though she had experienced some severe head trauma from her fall. By the time morning came, she had passed away. This continued the apparent trend in her past lives of pain and despair being closely associated with sexual activity and orgasm, potentially shedding some light on why she was experiencing her current issues.

Her final memory brought her to her present life. She was in her mother's womb. Her parents were engaged in intercourse, and she could feel her mother's clear revulsion towards her father during the ordeal. She could sense her mother's intentions; how she would never let him touch her again if she could help it. After this final intense, distressing and sexually distorted memory, Sarah was exhausted, but also felt a wave of contentment sweep over her. It was as if a weight had been lifted from her shoulders. Was she finally healed?

Sarah's case is not unique in the fact that her disorder dissipated after she had finally identified and recounted the origin of her trauma. In most instances, we find that once the origin of the issue that has carried over is identified and worked through emotionally, the individual is able to move on. In this case — soon after the final past life regression — Sarah Foster finally experienced her very first anxiety-free sexual encounter.

Case 3: A Clear Vision

In the last of the regression cases, we'll look into the story of one Amy Weiss, social worker and daughter to past life regression expert, Dr. Brian Weiss. What we find in her story is a relatively rare phenomenon when it comes to past life regression cases: A complete healing of a serious physical ailment.

At the young age of 25, Amy Weiss was diagnosed with a condition usually associated with old age, cataracts — a clouding of the lens in the eye leading to a gradual decrease in vision. Prior to this diagnosis, Amy had participated in numerous past life regression sessions, but had never experienced anything that could be considered a past life memory. This failure to respond to the process caused Amy to be very skeptical of the entire concept. So, when she agreed to participate in a hypnotic session shortly after her medical diagnosis, she went in with no small amount of disbelief. After struggling to enter trance for a while, she finally settled in.

The practitioner instructed her to allow her consciousness to go back to the origination of the symptoms which she now suffered from. To her astonishment, she was visualizing herself as an old man living a solitary life in what seemed to be the middle ages. This old man resided in a small hut and — for some unexplained reason — was perceived to be a kind of dark wizard by the surrounding townspeople. One day, stirred by some unknown motivation — possibly by fear having built up over time — the townspeople got together and decided to rid themselves of this "dark wizard".

A frenzied mob rushed his small hut bearing torches, and set fire to the structure with the man still inside. The violent flames caused severe burns to the man's eyes. Although he somehow survived the attack, he had lost his home and most of his possessions. As a result of the crippling disability, the man fell into a seemingly endless and deep depression.

As the session came to an end, Amy was guided by the therapist to seek some sort of dying wisdom from the past life she was envisioning. The overwhelming thought that she was left with was, "Sadness clouds the eyes." For Amy, this was a sort of a double entendre for her impending blindness, and the metaphoric blindness that depression was causing in her life. She was left with a sense of knowing that she had carried a part of the immense sadness of her past incarnation into her present.

Shortly after this past life regression, Amy met with her physicians. Much to her astonishment, her cataracts had completely vanished. The doctors had no medical explanation for what could have possibly caused this sudden disappearance of her condition, without any surgery or medical treatment. Amy Weiss, while baffled, was more than happy to accept this incredible anomaly.

Chapter 4:

<u>Stories from the East</u>

"I died as a mineral, and became a plant.

I died as a plant, and rose to animal.

I died as animal, and I was human.

Why should I fear?

When was I less by dying?"

- Rumi

Case 1: Markings

The first Eastern case we will explore is the story of a girl only known as "Mya", born outside of Yangon, Myanmar. The culture in Myanmar as a whole — being heavily influenced by Buddhism — does in fact embrace reincarnation as a true phenomenon. However, in the case of Mya, the family was not exactly thrilled about their daughter's stories.

Information of similar cases have been compiled by Dr. Ian Stevenson, who did remarkable work on the phenomenon of "experimental birthmarks". Stevenson coined the term in order to describe a particular practice found in several areas of Asia. In this custom, the corpse of a dying or recently departed individual is marked with a substance. The most commonly used is some simple soot. The belief is that if the individual is reborn, the newborn's body will show a birthmark corresponding to the placement of the mark on the departed person. The death mark then turns into a birthmark. The imprint on the body serves as a symbol of the individual spirit, confirming its identity through time. Stevenson discovered that this ritual practice was common in Asia, particularly in Thailand and Myanmar. During the 1990s, he reported 20 cases where experimental birthmarks were present. The story of a girl known only as Mya (her real name was withheld for reasons of privacy) is one such case.

Mya was born outside of Yangon, Myanmar to a family who did in fact believe in reincarnation, but with some amount of skepticism. We pick up the story 9 years before her birth — with the death of her maternal grandmother — who died of kidney disease at the age of 68. Upon her death, the daughter (Mya's mother) decided to carry out the aforementioned ritual where the body is marked with soot at the time of death. While the body was being marked — she prayed over the action — willing the marks to be carried by her deceased mother into her next life. The daughter of the deceased woman made two marks with soot, one on each ankle. Also present were several family members and a neighbor by the name of Ma Win Kyi.

Fast forward 9 years, to about a month before Mya's birth, when Mya's mother started having dreams about her deceased parent — Mya's grandmother. In these dreams, the grandmother asked several times if she could come live with the daughter again. Initially the answer was no, but in subsequent dreams the grandmother became much more insistent about her desire to live with her. Mya's mother eventually accepted her departed mother's desire, saying, "As you wish". At this point, the strange dreams completely stopped.

A month later, she became pregnant with Mya. She was later born without any complications. What was striking, however, was that she possessed two unusual birthmarks that just so happened to correspond perfectly with the ceremonial markings on her deceased grandmother's corpse. Though these marks eventually faded with time, what happened next was even more intriguing.

When Mya reached about One and a half years of age, she began asking for a specific mortar. Strangely, her grandmother owned precisely such a mortar. When Mya's uncle sustained an injury to his knee, she immediately suggested that the aforementioned mortar be used to pound the medicine that he needed, to put on his knee to be healed. Mya's grandmother had quite an extensive knowledge of medical treatments that the rest of the family didn't practice on a regular basis.

Another notable instance was when Mya began to ask for her jewelry around the age of two, and asking why the family had spent all the money she had left behind. What makes this particularly interesting is that the family had fallen on hard financial times long before the birth of Mya, and she had no knowledge of the fact that the grandmother had been very well off. The family completely was stunned and didn't know what to make of the toddler's astounding questions. Mya also had a striking behavioral trait that corresponded with the grandmother; the habit to eat with one leg hiked up in the chair. A strange quirk that only the grandmother of the family was ever known to do.

Like many children who are reported to have past life memories, Mya had a tendency to call her parents as well as her uncle and aunt by their given names as a child, something that goes against the cultural norm for children born in the region. It is considered a sign of deep disrespect that is not encouraged by the family or cultural norms. She also referred to her neighbor as "Daw Win Kyi" which was odd considering the rest of the family only referred to her as Ma Win Kyi. Nobody but the grandmother had ever referred to the neighbor as Daw Win Kyi, and Mya should have had no knowledge of this.

One of the last curious instances occurred during World War II, when Mya's cousin came to stay with the family. Mya was then five years old. Immediately upon meeting for the first time, she referred to her cousin as "Baby", which is a name that only the grandmother used for the cousin. The rest of the family never referred to the cousin by this nickname.

By this point in Mya's life, the family was beginning to become distressed by their child's close association with the deceased grandmother. The constant recounting of the grandmother's life was turning into a point of contention for the family. Because of this, the family resolved to begin feeding Mya a lot of eggs. In their culture, this was believed to aid in the forgetting of a past incarnation. As Mya became older — and the family continued to discourage the talk of her supposed previous life as her granny — she recounted these memories less and less, until she only spoke of them in instances of heightened emotional distress.

Case 2: Homesick

Here we have a case of a child with past life memories that were exceptionally vivid and clear. The parents had a loose belief in reincarnation, but were initially skeptical when their child began recounting the memories of an apparently different person.

An Indian boy named Toran "Titu" Singh started speaking of his "other family" around the age of two. As he grew older, he began talking about "the shop", "Uma" and "TV". He repeated this incessantly, which made his parents very confused. As he became better at talking, however, he started relaying his memories in greater detail. He claimed that he was once a small business owner in Agra, a populous city in the state of Uttar Pradesh, in the northern region in India.

He remembered owning a shop that sold TVs, video equipment and radios. Titu even recalled that his full name was *Suresh Verma*, and that he had two small children together with his wife, Uma. He could also name one of his previous brothers, Raja Babu, and his sister, Susheela. Titu had a tendency to cry from time to time, saying that he was homesick and wanted to go back to Agra. Eventually, he became more and more insistent. One day, when the longing became too much to bear, he put some clothes into a bag and threatened to run away from home.

Titu would often brag to his older brother about how he was a smuggler, and that he made a decent amount of money between running the shop and selling smuggled goods. His family initially dismissed all of his stories as the ramblings of a child with an overactive imagination. However — as the child grew — his older brother decided on a whim to attempt to verify his sibling's extraordinary claims.

During the older brother's travel to Agra, he discovered that there was indeed a shop there — much like the one his younger brother described — which was owned by a family named Verma. The person who ran the shop just so happened to be a widow by the name of Uma. The young man told the widow the story about how his younger brother suddenly began to speak of her shop and family in great detail. Initially, Uma was skeptical and slightly weirded out by the whole scenario. Still, after some time spent dwelling on the idea, she decided to go and investigate these claims for herself. Together with the deceased Suresh's parents and three brothers, she traveled to the Singh's village.

As Uma showed up at the Singh household — completely unannounced — she was greeted by Titu who immediately recognized her. He shouted happily that his "other family" had come to visit him at last. When the Singh family invited them in, Titu insisted that Uma had to sit close to him. She thought this was quite a strange request coming from a five-year-old boy. Then, he proceeded to ask about the children's wellbeing, which startled her. He went on to completely floor the widow by recounting a story of a family outing they had gone on in the past, where he had given her some particular sweets. This was a story that only Suresh could have possibly known about. He also spoke of how he had buried gold in a hole inside the house. Now, whether or not the gold was ever found is anybody's guess, the family didn't speak of it openly (which was probably for the better).

After their meeting, it was decided that Titu should be allowed to travel to Agra, and his family arranged the trip with the help of Uma Verma. Prior to Titu's arrival, the Verma family — understandably skeptical — had arranged for Titu to be thoroughly tested regarding his extraordinary claims. When Titu arrived in Agra, he was to be brought to an area where the Verma children were playing in a group of many other kids. To everyone's astonishment, Titu pointed out the Verma children immediately upon seeing them, compelling them to come and play with him. After a day spent playing and catching up with the kids, Titu was taken to the Verma family's shop, where he promptly pointed out a number of changes that had been made since his life as Suresh. According to Uma Verma, all of the changes were accurately spotted.

When recounting the end of his life as Suresh, Titu gave correct details of what had occurred the night of his death, on August 28, 1983. He spoke of how he was murdered by a gunman while sitting in his car, after having returned home from a long day at work. What was even more remarkable was that on Titu's head there were birthmarks that precisely corresponded with the entry and exit wounds of the bullet that killed Suresh. With this preponderance of evidence, both of the families had seen enough to believe that Titu Singh was in fact the reincarnation of Suresh Verma. They decided to stay in touch, and the two families formed a close relationship.

With the help of his parents, Titu provided the details of his murder to the courts in Agra. A businessman by the name of Sedick Johaadien was the one who shot him, he said, along with another unidentified accomplice. When Agra police confronted Sedick, he became visibly distressed and — after a long session of questioning — he eventually confessed to the murder. In the end, Titu was able to convince the court that he indeed was the reincarnation of Suresh Verma.

The fact that Titu managed to get the police and judicial system involved, makes this one of the most heavily documented cases of past life memory ever recorded. The case was later reported in the London-based magazine *Reincarnation International*. BBC (British Broadcasting Corporation) also televised Titu's story on a news program called *Forty Minutes* in 1990.

Case 3: Echoes in Urdu

Naresh Kumar was born in February of 1981 in the small village of Baznagar, located in the Etah district in the Indian state of Uttar Pradesh. Otherwise a perfectly healthy child, he was born with a strange birth defect which appeared as a slightly depressed area on the right side of his chest. While it looked somewhat troublesome to the naked eye, the doctors concluded that it posed no threat to his health.

Naresh lived together with his father Guruprasad, and his mother, Bishwana. As Hindus, they maintained an otherwise ordinary life as a lower middle class family. When Naresh started speaking at one year of age, however, things took a turn for the strange. He began talking about "Kakori", which is a town in the Lucknow district, in another part of Uttar Pradesh. This town is known for its prominence of Urdu poetry, literature and the *Qadiriya-Qalandari* Sufi Order. This baffled his parents, who had no connection to the town or its particular Islamic culture whatsoever. A few weeks later, he added the word "kharkhara" — which was a local term meaning *horse cart*.

When Naresh reached two years of age, his parents became stunned as he assumed the posture of kneeling down and voicing the *Namaz* — which is a Muslim prayer known as *Salah* in Arabic. He would usually perform this prayer by himself, stopping if he noticed anyone observing him. When playing, he would often pretend to drive the horse cart of which he spoke. He would tie a rope to his bunk — which would serve as the cart — and then he would make different sounds, as if he was ordering horses to continue forward.

In addition to these oddities, Naresh would frequently communicate with a few specific words of Urdu, a language which his family did not speak. When he reached four years of age, Naresh could finally start to explain the reason for his curious behavior. He started telling his family about another lifetime, when he was a Muslim who lived in Kakori. He stated that he was transporting mangoes in a horse cart, when it collided violently with a tractor. This brought him a great injury which caused his body to cease functioning. The next thing he remembered was being a small child once again.

As reincarnation is more accepted in Indian society, his family encouraged Naresh to tell people about his previous life. Highly intrigued, people in the village would often ask him questions, which he would answer with enthusiasm. As he started venturing outside in the village, he would eventually come to recognize a familiar face.

Haider Ali was a deeply religious Sufi ascetic who would travel to Baznagar every Thursday, where he prayed for the locals and gathered alms and donations which sustained him. As soon as Naresh spotted him, he started calling him "abba", which means father. He would follow the ascetic man all around the village — claiming he was his son — saying that he wanted to return home to Kakori with him. Haider Ali heard clearly what Naresh was saying, but chose to ignore the boy's wild claims. After all, his Islamic faith did not teach him about reincarnation, and his Muslim community would certainly criticize him for entertaining such an idea.

Saddened by the rejection, Naresh started begging his family to go with him to Kakori. His mother, Bishwana, determined to ask Haider Ali for his help, seeing as he was from the town. Startled about the proposal, Ali chose to not get involved, and advised Bishwana to take the boy to the grave of a Muslim saint instead. This — he believed — would get Naresh to stop talking about his alleged memories. She took his advice and visited the gravesite, but nothing changed. Naresh still insisted on visiting his old home. Increasingly frustrated, he started travelling down the road by himself, before his father eventually intercepted him and got him back to the village. After this incident, his father Guruprasad decided that enough was enough. He finally agreed take Naresh to the town he wouldn't stop talking about. Together with some friends from the village, they arrived in Kakori, and went to the house where a boy named Mushir Ali, son of the Sufi ascetic Haider Ali, had lived.

Once they got inside, Naresh gave a laid-back tour of what he claimed was his house, seemingly familiar with every nook and cranny of the building. While both the group from his village and the Ali family looked on, Naresh identified numerous objects which belonged to Mushir — including his cap and the contents of a locked suitcase. Naresh also correctly named the members of Mushir Ali's immediate family, as well as a number of his close relatives and friends.

Remarkably, he also accurately described a bank account and all of its contents, which the Ali family had at the time of his death — as well as mentioning the name of a person who owed Mushir money. Both of these claims were verified by the Ali family, adding that the money was paid back after Mushir died. Based on his confident behavior, vivid descriptions and accurate identifications, the Ali family — including the wary

Haider — accepted Naresh as the reincarnation of their son Mushir Ali.

Dr. Satwant Pasricha, the head of Department of Clinical Psychology at NIMHANS (National Institute of Mental Health and Neurosciences at Bangalore), was assigned to investigate Naresh's story. She worked with Ian Stevenson's group at the University of Virginia, and investigated around 500 cases of past life memory through her career. She detailed the life and death of Mushir Ali, and found striking correlations between him and the statements of Naresh Kumar.

Mushar Ali lived together with his family in the town of Kakori. He, like the rest of his family, was Sunni Muslim. He was the one who brought in the most money by selling different kinds of fruits and vegetables at various markets in the area. In the early morning of June 30, 1980, Mushir Ali was transporting mangoes to different markets in the Lucknow district. He was driving a horse cart which he had rented for the day. When he was about 1.5 miles from Kakori, a tractor suddenly crashed with his cart at full speed. The violent crash resulted in several fractures of the ribs on the right side of his body, which made him quickly bleed out and die. He was 25 years old at the time of death.

When closely examined, the details of Mushar's life and death which were provided by Naresh proved to be stunningly accurate. The vivid descriptions of the house and village, the bank account and its contents, the names of Mushar's family and friends, and the words spoken in Urdu together with the spontaneous Islamic prayer. Additionally, Naresh's strange birth defect aligned perfectly with the deadly wound which

Mushar suffered during the collision. All things considered, Naresh made quite a convincing case for the validity of his remarkable story.

Case 4: Out of the Fire

A girl named Mithilesh Singh was born in Agra, India in 1975. She had a father named Navratan and a mother named Rajwati. Mithilesh had three siblings, one of which was her younger sister, Meena, who Mithilesh had a very close connection with. Her maternal aunt — Ganga Bai — was also close to her heart.

Of all the Singh's children, Mithilesh was the only one who consistently underperformed at school. In order to help her pass the high school's final examinations, her parents decided to send her to live with her older cousin — Virender — who lived in a village called Bhalaul. Their intention was that another family member in the area — who worked as a teacher — would assist Mithilesh in getting ready for the exams. Also sharing the space of Virender's home was his wife, Bimla, and his mother, Shakuntala.

Shakuntala would prove to be a highly domineering person, always asserting her will over the other women while frequently talking down to them. She had a special kind of contempt for Bimla, who she did not feel was good enough to be paired with her son. Through Shakuntala's reign of terror, Bimla and Mithilesh grew very close as they found shelter in each other's company.

While studying in Bhalaul, Mithilesh found herself falling deeply in love with a local boy. When her parents found out about the relationship, they voiced their disapproval and forbid Mithilesh from being with her newfound lover. The reason for their insistent objection was that the boy was of a lower "caste". The Indian caste system is a system of social stratification which assigns particularly negative traits to the unfortunate ones at the bottom of the societal pyramid. In many cases, they are even thought of as inherently "unclean", and that they should not even be touched by individuals of the higher castes. Due to the boy's placement in this system, him and Mithilesh were harshly separated, which broke Mithilesh's heart. She went into a deep, seemingly endless depression.

In early October of 1991, Mithilesh's aunt and mother came to visit her in Bhalaul. They went on a ride in a pony cart together, discussing Mithilesh's plans for the future, or — more likely — the family's plans for her future. This apparently pushed the depressed Mithilesh over the edge. When they arrived at Virender's house, she suddenly poured a can of kerosene over her head and then ignited the fluid, setting fire to her whole upper body. She panicked due to the intense pain and ran towards Bimla for help. Bimla was pregnant at the time, and became horrified at the sight of a hysterical Mithilesh engulfed in flames running towards her. In a moment of fear, she pushed her back and got out of the room.

Mithilesh's aunt and mother finally managed to extinguish the fire, and rushed Mithilesh to a nearby hospital. Except for her feet and waist, her entire body had been severely burned. Despite the doctors' best efforts, her injuries proved to be fatal. She was only 16 years old when she died. About a month after Mithilesh's horrific suicide, Rajwati — her mother — had a vivid dream which told her that Mithilesh would soon be returning to the family in a new body. Later that year, Bimla Singh birthed a baby girl. She was given the name Rajani.

When Rajani's mother and grandmother were taking care of her a few days after the birth, they noticed several red marks on her head. Soon after, they discovered additional red marks which covered most of her upper body as well, although the marks on the head were the most prominent. Rajwati came to see the baby and observed the red birth marks which covered the child's body. Based on these marks and the vivid dream about Mithilesh returning to the family, Rajwati thought that Rajani could be the reincarnation of her daughter.

After learning to talk properly, Rajani would continuously ask for Meena, who was the younger sister of Mithilesh. Before even getting to know the overbearing Shakuntala, she showed great fear towards the woman, and would rather avoid her. When Rajani reached four years of age, she was taken to the house where Mithilesh had lived. She showed clear signs of familiarity with both the house and the family members there, and she could identify them all by name. She was also particularly affectionate towards Mithilesh's favored aunt, Ganga Bai.

Rajani would frequently insist on being called Mithilesh, and she stated that her mother was Rajwati, and that her father was Navratan. She always addressed them as such each time they met. According to Dr. Pasricha (the same investigator as in the Mushir/Naresh story), who was investigating the case, there was a strong similarity in facial features between Rajani and a young Mithilesh, which included the noteworthy large and clear eyes. The personality traits of the two girls were also virtually identical.

Pasricha also noted the nature of Rajani's strange birthmarks, which included a location on the right side of the child's head that was hairless and lighter in color than the rest of her body. The red areas also covered Rajani's shoulder and back, but the lower body was completely clear, which matched the marks on Mithilesh's burned body. Similar to birth marks found on other allegedly reincarnated children, Rajani's red marks eventually disappeared completely as she got older.

So, what can we say about this case?

While Rajani's face was similar to Mithilesh, some would attribute this to the relatively close genetic relationship between the two girls. This is in contrast to most other reincarnation cases, where strong facial similarities can be seen between two people whose physical bodies had no immediate genetic ties. One could also argue that Mithilesh's mother — Rajwati — planted ideas in Rajani's head due to wishful thinking, as she wanted her daughter back.

On the other hand, the identical personalities, the familiarity of the old house, Rajwati's precognitive dream, Rajani's correct naming of Mithilesh's family and the clear aversion towards Shakuntala suggests otherwise.

The most interesting part of this story, however, is the red birth marks on Rajani's upper body. How likely is it that a girl who is alleged to be the reincarnation of another deceased girl, possesses birth marks which perfectly match both the color and location of the dead girl's burn marks? When you add this fact to Rajani's aforementioned traits, the chance of it all being nothing more than chance seems highly unlikely.

Case 5: The Crash

Ahmet Delibalta was a man from Adana, a major city in the southern part of Turkey. He initially married a woman named Mihriban and had three children with her. Later, he also took a second wife, Fehime. Ahmet was a businessman, and was passionate about running his own nightclub, *Havuz*. He was great with finances, and used some of the profits from the club to eventually open a bakery as well. He became rather successful at his business ventures, and enjoyed an above average lifestyle — living in a large house, eating well and wearing fine clothing.

Ahmet travelled to Istanbul in 1962, searching for a female singer for his nightclub in Adana. His second wife Fehime was pregnant at the time of his departure. Once he arrived in Istanbul, he quickly discovered a talented woman named Rengin Arda, who he hired. While Ahmet and his newly hired singer were on a flight back to Adana — on March 8, 1962 — their plane crashed in a remote area of the snowy Toros Mountains. At first it was assumed that all passengers died in the impact. This later turned out to be false.

It took the assigned rescue operation several days before reaching the wreckage, whereupon it was discovered that some of the passengers had survived the crash, though they were not found in the immediate vicinity. Investigators eventually found all of the missing victims, scattered throughout the frozen and rugged terrain. They had all frozen to death. One of the ice-cold corpses belonged to Ahmet Delibalta. He was 35 years old at the time of death.

When the first batch of bodies were brought down from the mountain — the victims of the impact of the plane crash — there was a mishap when identifying the corpse of a man. When Ahmet's younger brother was asked to identify him, he couldn't bare himself to look at what he thought was the lifeless body of his deceased sibling. Instead, he requested to be shown the clothing which covered the departed, whereupon he confirmed that the apparel belonged to his brother.

Unbeknownst to Ahmet's brother, however, was that the body belonged to another man. Ahmet's corpse, at the time, was laying somewhere in the wilderness of the Toros Mountains. Nevertheless, the body of this unknown man was buried in a graveyard under the name of Ahmet Delibalta. It was not until the rest of the bodies were recovered that the grievous error was discovered. Luckily, Ahmet was wearing an identity card when he passed. Consequently, the unknown man's corpse was unearthed and reburied elsewhere, and Ahmet's body was properly laid to rest.

A woman named Latife Kilic lived in Adana — near where Ahmet had lived — together with her husband Yusef. In the week before Ahmet's plane crashed in the mountains, she had an intense and vivid dream. In this vision, Ahmet greeted her. Latife knew Ahmet only by seeing him around his club, Havuz. They had not even formally introduced themselves to each other. Still — in this highly intimate dream — Ahmet gave her a wrapped gift, and then laid down on the bed between Latife and her husband. When she woke in the morning, Latife asked Yusef,

"What does that nightclub man want at our place?".

She was pregnant at the time of the dream, and approaching term. Approximately two weeks after — on march 13, 1962, she delivered a boy. The boy was named Erkan, and would prove to be quite different from all of his 14 siblings.

Since his birth, Erkan was shown to have an immense fear of airplanes. This phobia was triggered both by seeing an airplane and/or hearing their engines. Whenever this set him off, he would seek out the protection of his mother or hide under his bed until the perceived threat had passed. This lasted until he reached three years of age.

When interviewed by Dr, Ian Stevenson, Latife mentioned that Erkan greatly enjoyed pretending that he was the owner of a nightclub. He would assign different roles to the kids in the neighborhood, and handed one of them a stick which was meant to represent a microphone. He could also be seen setting out chairs and tables for potential patrons. Erkan was behaving quite confident and satisfied while playing in this way, showing extraordinary talent in organization and leadership at such a young age.

As soon as Erkan learned how to talk — between two and three years of age — he told Latife that she was not his actual mother. This act — a child disowning one or both parents, as we have seen previously — is a common feature in past life memory cases. He requested that she bring him to his real mother and that he see his wife again. Erkan also declared that his actual name was Ahmet. He also mentioned that he owned a bakery, and a nightclub called *Havuz*.

Soon after these startling statements, he went on to describe the details of his death in his past lifetime as Ahmet. He casually told Latife that he had travelled to Istanbul to look for a singer for his club. He then told her about the plane crash in the Toros Mountains. Erkan explained that he did not die in the crash itself, but froze to death later. Ian Stevenson — who was investigating this case — found this statement particularly intriguing, as everyone close to Erkan thought that all of the victims had died in the impact of the crash. Only a few people who were closely involved with the investigation knew that some of the passengers froze to death afterwards.

Additionally, Erkan also somehow knew that his body was initially confused with another, unknown man. Ahmet's family was apparently greatly ashamed of the incident, and kept it entirely to themselves. Erkan's knowledge of this confusion regarding the corpses implies that he could observe his body after passing on — an often reported feature of other reincarnation cases (e.g. the story of Taru Jarvi) as well as many near-death experiences.

When Erkan was three years of age, he made statements where he would name several close relatives of Ahmet Delibalta. He named his mother, father, his two sons, his daughter, his sister and his mother-in-law. When Stevenson checked with the Delibalta family, he found that all of the names given were 100% correct. Erkan would also talk often and warmly about his wife, Mihriban, and that he had an additional wife called Fehime. He admitted that he favored Mihriban's company over Fehime, a fact that was verified by Ahmet's brother-in-law.

One day, Erkan demonstrated a strong wish to visit the main locales of his previous lifetime. He snuck out of the house one quiet evening, and walked to the home of Ahmet Delibalta by himself, which was no more than 200 yards or so away from the Kilics' household. Mihriban — Ahmet's widow — was still living in the house, and he recognized her immediately. He introduced himself to her, and casually strolled around inside the building. Latife later met with Mihriban and talked to her about her son's unusual claims.

As Erkan continued to run into the Delibalta family, he became good friends with one of Ahmet's sons, Ali. They would play together for hours on end, and would often create quite a bit of noise. One time, when Latife tried to send Ali away, Erkan would get between them and say to her, "Stop, that's my son", whereupon she gave in and let them continue playing. A neighbor told Ian Stevenson that Erkan would embrace Ali not as a playmate, but as a son.

Erkan would continue to sneak out of the house to visit his alleged past wife, where he would often stay until late at night — to the dismay of his parents. Unfortunately, Latife found the frequent trips of his so distressing that she started beating him to stop him from going back. Mihriban, however, had a sister who lived just across the street from the Kilic family. When she came to visit her, she took the children with her as well. On these occasions, Erkan would climb up onto the roof and simply sit there and observe them from a distance. When his siblings questioned him about his activities, he answered, "I am watching my wife and children".

Another day, Erkan asked if he could go and visit his other mother. Latife said that she didn't know where his mother lived. Erkan insisted that he could show the way to her house himself. Latife allowed him to take the lead, and so he led her about 220 yards away, to a home next door to a bakery. Not only was this the home of Ahmet Delibalta's mother, but the bakery next to the home was the one which was owned by Ahmet. Erkan would come to repeatedly visit this bakery, and confidently told the workers there that he was the rightful owner of the business. One worker became completely convinced that Erkan was the reincarnation of Ahmet, and gave him free bread whenever he would visit.

The singer who died in the same plane crash as Ahmet on the way from Istanbul, had been in Adana once before. A local hairdresser who she went to had taken a picture with her while she was on this trip. When this hairdresser heard about Erkan's stories of reincarnation, she approached the Kilic family and requested to perform her own little test. She brought out the photograph of her and Rengin Arda, the singer, and asked Erkan who the ladies in the picture were. Erkan quickly replied that the picture was of her and the singer. Interestingly, no one else in the Kilic family had even heard about the singer from Istanbul.

Two especially strange events took place when Erkan was around four years old. The first oddity emerged when he mentioned that — while he was still Ahmet — he and a close friend of his, named Mithat, exchanged watches, and that Mithat was still in possession of his wristwatch. This watch — he added — had teeth marks on it from Ahmet's children. Dr. Ian Stevenson decided to contact Mithat, who confirmed that he had indeed exchanged watches with Ahmet. He added that it was highly unlikely that anyone else could have known about

66

this fact. When Stevenson inspected the wristwatch, he found the teeth marks on its case, perfectly matching Erkan's description.

A second anomalous remark came short after, when Erkan said that — in his previous life — he had stolen a tray from his parents. He sold the tray in order to get money for a football game. He added that he sold the tray for 25 kurus (a Turkish currency subunit). This particular episode was later confirmed by another of Ahmet's friends, Selim Ozel. This took place when Ahmet was 15 years old, a whole 20 years before his death in the Toros Mountains. When Selim met Erkan for the first time, he asked if anyone else went with them to the football game. Erkan quickly responded that there was a third boy called Tevfic who accompanied them. This was confirmed by Selim as being correct. He added that they had never told anyone else about the incident, in fear of potential retaliation.

All in all, this is one of the most detailed cases which Ian Stevenson investigated during his travels. It is interesting to note that the Kilic family neither believed nor was interested in reincarnation prior to Erkan's revelations. Nor did his surroundings in Turkey provide any notable inspiration for his stories. When you consider all of the completely correct statements Erkan made about Ahmet's life — his cause of death, his businesses, his life experiences, his possessions, his family and friends — the chance of it all being a coincidence seems infinitesimal.

Something which stands out in this story compared to the typical past life memory case, is the incredibly small window of time between the person's death and rebirth, which was merely two weeks or so. The average interval between death and rebirth in Stevenson's published cases, on the other hand, is two *years*. This certainly brings up two specific questions about the process of dying and the time it takes to enter into a new body. How early and how late?

Most of the stories we have covered in this book only saw the light of day thanks to Dr. Ian Stevenson and his colleagues' tremendous research initiatives. While Stevenson's efforts are continued by people like Jim B. Tucker at the University of Virginia, the generous donation of Chester Carlson has long since been used to its fullest. The resources needed for any serious, full-time investigative effort into reincarnation cases is — at the moment — sorely missing.

How many stories have passed us by? How many baffling cases of past life memories are taking place right at this moment?

As there are currently some serious efforts being made towards bridging the gap between spirituality and science, we can only hope that — eventually — there will be funding for future endeavors similar to Stevenson's. Illuminating the reality of reincarnation will undoubtedly assist us in better contemplating the nature of this mystery we call existence.

Sources used

- "Children's Past Life Memories", Interview with Dr. Jim Tucker by Coast to Coast AM, August 31, 2005.
From: http://www.coasttocoastam.com/show/2005/08/31

- "Children's Past Lives", Interview with Dr. Jim Tucker by Coast to Coast AM, December 22, 2013.
From: http://www.coasttocoastam.com/show/2013/12/22

- "Reincarnation, Part One: The Research of Ian Stevenson, with Walter Semkiw", Interview on "New Thinking Allowed", hosted by Jeffrey Mishlove, PhD.
From: https://www.youtube.com/watch?v=3VvX3P69HX8

- "Reincarnation, Part Two: Cases of Xenoglossy, with Walter Semkiw", Interview on "New Thinking Allowed", hosted by Jeffrey Mishlove, PhD.
From: https://www.youtube.com/watch?v=h2mmEYEzwjo

- "Reincarnation, Part Three: Identifying Past Lives, with Walter Semkiw", Interview on "New Thinking Allowed", hosted by Jeffrey Mishlove, PhD.
From: https://www.youtube.com/watch?v=yIFk4EpojKc

- "English Schoolboy Lived Before – As Nazi Airman", Weekly World News, May 28, 2002.

- "The uncanny case of Carl Edon", Evening Gazette, 22 Jul 2013.
From: http://www.gazettelive.co.uk/news/local-news/uncanny-case-carl-edon-3857619

- "Chilling Reincarnation Stories: Children Who Lived Before".
From: http://www.rd.com/health/conditions/chilling-reincarnation-stories/

- "Past Life Story of an African Tribesman", article by Walter Semkiw, M.D.
From: http://www.iisis.net/index.php%3Fpage%3Dsemkiw-ian-stevenson-reincarantion-race-change-african-elisabeth-gedeon-haich-initiation%26hl%3Den_US

- "Premier exemple de réincarnation : Gédéon Haich", Trouver le Bonheur.
From: http://laveritesurlebonheur.com/index.php/une-vie-c-est-trop-peu-vous-voulez-dire-reincarne/premier-exemple-de-reincarnation-gedeon-haich

- Capretto, L. "Dr. Brian Weiss' Daughter, Amy, Recalls Experience with Past-Life Regression".
From: http://www.huffingtonpost.com/2013/06/04/past-life-regression-brian-weiss-daughter-amy_n_3380356.html

- "Past Life Regression Therapy Case Studies: Past Life Experiences, Evidence, Regressions, Resolution."
From:
http://www.pastlifetherapycenter.com/Past_Life_Therapy_Center_Case_Studies_Regression.html

- "Scientific probe into the realm of unknown throws up new evidence on paranormal phenomena".
From: http://indiatoday.intoday.in/story/scientific-probe-into-the-realm-of-unknown-throws-up-new-evidence-on-paranormal-phenomena/1/330132.html

- "Scientific evidence for reincarnation", lecture by Dr. Ian Stevenson, at Jordan Hall Auditorium, University of Virginia.
From: https://www.youtube.com/watch?v=PbWMEWubrk0

- "Forty Minutes" – Reincarnation episode, (BBC documentary, 1990).

- "Double Birthmarks: The Case Of Titu", Article by Carol Bowman
From: http://www.carolbowman.com/library/double-birthmarks/

- "Past Lives and evidence of Reincarnation", Article by Supernatural Magazine.
From: http://supernaturalmagazine.com/articles/past-lives-and-evidence-of-reincarnation

- "In Search of the Dead", (BBC documentary series, 1992).

- "Past Lives: Stories of Reincarnation", (Discovery Channel Documentary, 2003).

- "Indian Cases of the Reincarnation Type Two Generations Apart", Journal by Dr. Ian Stevenson and Satwant Pasricha, University of Virginia.
From: https://med.virginia.edu/perceptual-studies/wp-content/uploads/sites/267/2015/11/STE25.pdf

- "5th Dimension – Secrets of The Supernatural", (Discovery Channel documentary, 2006).

- "Conversations/Dr. Ian Stevenson; You May Be Reading This In Some Future Past Life", The New York Times, September 26, 1999.
From: http://www.nytimes.com/1999/09/26/weekinreview/conversations-dr-ian-stevenson-you-may-be-reading-this-in-some-future-past-life.html?pagewanted=all

- "Ian Stevenson; Sought To Document Memories of Past Lives in Children", The Washington Post, February 11, 2007.
From: http://www.washingtonpost.com/wp-dyn/content/article/2007/02/10/AR2007021001393.html

- "Afterlife: Are We 'Skeptics' Really Just Cynics?", Article by Jesse Bering, Scientific American, November 2, 2013.
From: http://blogs.scientificamerican.com/bering-in-mind/ian-stevensone28099s-case-for-the-afterlife-are-we-e28098skepticse28099-really-just-cynics/

- "Cases of the Reincarnation Type in Northern India With Birthmarks and Birth Defects", by Satwant K. Pasricha.
From: http://documents.mx/documents/reincarnation-pasricha.html

- "Omni Magazine Interview with Dr. Ian Stevenson", by Meryle Secrest, 1988.
From: http://www.carolbowman.com/dr-ian-stevenson/omni-magazine-interview/

- "Ian Stevenson and Cases of the Reincarnation Type", Essay by Jim B. Tucker, M.D., 2008.
From: https://med.virginia.edu/perceptual-studies/wp-content /uploads/sites/267/2015/11/ REI36Tucker-1.pdf

- "Professor Ian Stevenson", Obituary by The Telegraph, February 12, 2007.
From: http://www.telegraph.co.uk/news/obituaries/1542356/Professor-Ian-Stevenson.html

- "Ian Pretyman Stevenson", Obituary by The BMJ, March 29, 2007.
From: http://www.bmj.com/rapid-response/2011/11/01/professor-ian-stevenson-emperor-parapsychology

- "Journal of Scientific Exploration", Volume 22, Number 1, University of Virginia, 2008.
From: https://med.virginia.edu/perceptual-studies/wp-content/uploads/sites/267/2015/11/jse-22-1-2008.pdf

"The creation is vast.

Mysteries abound.

Keep the mind clear.

What is sought shall be found."

CPSIA information can be obtained
at www.ICGtesting.com
Printed in the USA
LVOW13s1514240117
522003LV00011BA/899/P

9 781530 631377